Poetic

Peace

A Compilation of poetry for all

By Haley Belinda.

6.   For further details, contact the publisher at the address above.

7.   First Edition

8.   ISBN 978-1-64440-658-8

9.   Printed by the supplier

Preface

Welcome to Haley Belinda's poetry collection.

Haley has chosen a selection from the many

poems she has written since 2006.

Some of the poems form stories, others are

tributes to family.

There are a select few which have appeared in

competitions but mostly these have not been

published before.

Published exclusively in this book.

Enjoy.

Dedications &

Acknowledgments

To My late Mother and Father (Amazing

parents')

To my sisters, nieces and nephews

To my children for putting up with me

reciting.

To my grandchildren for been a pleasure,

sweet blessings

To my auntie's for being rocks

To The Lord My God in heaven for the gift.

.

Table of Contents

Haley Belinda / A Compilation

Chapter 1-A variety

Poetic Peace

Performance enhancements

Of carefully chosen and

Extraordinary words.

Tributes are made

Inspiring the writers

Collections of poetry.

Poetically creating imagery,

Exhibiting carefully!

Attributes are

Chosen to create

Endearing memories and peace.

In the Nick of Time

Time on earth is measured,
Measured by the sun,
Sun brings lots of happiness,
Happiness for one.

One is the first of numbers,
Numbers are found on clocks,
Clocks measure time,
Time says: Tick-tock, tick-tock,

Tick-tock comes from a pendulum,
Pendulum that swings,
Swings into action,
Action from a spring,

Spring is a season,
Season of life's prime,
Prime life is precious,
Precious because of time...

Time on earth is measured,
Measured by the sun,
Sun brings lots of happiness,
Happiness for one.

Dawn versus the Sunset

Glorious sunrise.

Yellow it rests on pale blue.

Flames fringe the night blinds...

Precious

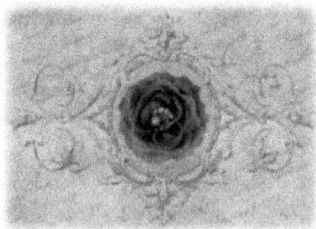

Preciously

Reviewing

Events

Curating

Interesting

Opinions

Unimaginable

Success

Tired Eyes Can't Sleep

It was cold but the moon,

Was bright,

Late December,

The stars were alight,

My bedroom was 'cozy',

All are asleep,

Except for me!

Eyes tired can't sleep!

Haley Belinda / A Compilation

My dogs, they are huddled,

One of them snores!

My children are quiet,

Behind their doors,

But out of the window,

And down the street,

I could hear someone launching,

The pavement did meet!

Mrs. Paloma flew out of the door,

To check the person,

Laid flat on the floor!

"Are you Okay? Come on, let's see?"

So, they went for a natter,

A cup of tea!

My eyes are still tired,

But instead of being dozy,

I admired the sky,

I continued to nosy.

It was now four a.m.

There was a heck of a crash,

This time! It was a poor old lass!

Was it the ice? Or just her own feet?

No! The elastic had broken,

Now left her seat!

Haley Belinda / A Compilation

Oh dear, I thought;

That was a fright!

Not to mention,

An awkward sight!

I' m glad Miss Dumbarton was just going in,

When those awake,

Heard the terrible 'din'.

At least the old lass,

Had nothing fractured,

Except perhaps her pride,

With the rotten elastic.

The night was now quiet,

There was nothing to see,

A few blowing branches swaying on the

trees,

My Eyes are still tired, time for defeat.

I laid back down and went to sleep.

World War Games

The stillness and quiet

Of night as it approaches dawn. Soon—

there is some chirping from outside

near the lawn.

Miles away is CONTRAST:

There is banging and wailing,

children all forlorn.

Not a nice reception for those,

this coming dawn.

Haley Belinda / A Compilation

'Abba'! Father, I shout,
"bring your hand out, heal this worldly
mess?"
"Use your POWER, Stop the humans using
theirs, get RID of the distress!"

BANG! Devastation and desolation all
around.
NOWHERE to walk on this human carpet on
the ground.

I heard the VOICE! It said,
"I am coming, my child, just so many souls
left to save!
Like any Father; I don't want to leave a child
stuck in the grave."

Oh, please! Stop! All you leaders,

it's NOT a game.

"Take your fingers off the buttons!"

It's fathers, mothers, children, sisters and

brothers.

NOT TOY SOLDIERS, at stake!

Historic Village

As I drove through the village,

I did surmise,

Thousands of people have lived and died,

I looked at the changes which had arrived

from the new modern buildings

—and Victorian alike!

If only these magnificent buildings could

speak,

What a tale of history they could repeat,

The loves, the lost, the good and the bad

Oh, what a tale could be had?

So many life stories, year upon a year,

As we live, grow and die and disappear.

Accident and Emergency— A Moral

The noise of a busy department.

Even in the early hours too.
They keep on walking and working;
Is it him next or you?

Don't go to the door or the toilet,
Or be stranded with sticks in a chair!
Or you find yourself at the back of the
queue,
Thinking, Hey! That's unfair!

Haley Belinda / A Compilation

You arrive in an ambulance wheelchair,
Feeling ill and all forlorn,

It's Friday and you meet an old friend,
Now you're wishing you could pole vault—
Down the road!!!

But, the laughter brings such good healing,
And gosh! Such fresh air.
As we got down to reminiscing,
We had been teenagers with dare!

I remembered the time we went dancing,
The Teeny-bopper two-hour club!
We didn't know how we would get there,
With blisters and toes that were stubbed.

You said. "Hey! There's my uncle?"

He stopped!

I couldn't believe what I saw.

Next, we' re on the back of a milk cart;

He took us right up to the door!

Back to the A and E department,

Almost everyone had gone.

I'd sat there in my wheelchair,

Still tight chested and waiting too long!

The moral: Don't make assumptions
It's not that folk don't care!
It's not that you ignored the call!
Or that you just were not there!

Remember the people in wheelchairs,
Or the ones who are scared 'on sticks'
They just cannot shout!
"I am coming!" Tight chested—
They cannot be quick.

Chapter two Faith

For the Love of a Red Rose

Red Rose,

Glistens with rain.

Glorious in beauty,

Fine petals adorn. Sharp, bleeding,

God's LOVE.

Faith

I sat feeling weary

My bones felt like a ton.

My words just whispered

from my tongue.

Faith, where are you?

Just a dark week

My Lord, I did seek,

My child almost achieved

her ill-fated deed.

Faith, I need you.

We share in your suffering

And I am gratified,

This needs no buffering.

as I am satisfied.

Faith, I see you.

I hold your word,

I need your GRACE

I have concurred

Faith, I'm forgiven...

The sword of your spirit

Lifts my soul

I do not cry but laugh,

I am whole.

Faith, you are Faithful.

Blessed are we,

who do not see,

But accept with you;

You will always BE.

Faith, a Saviour.

An Artistic Masterpiece

A glorious display of colours

A cascade of glory

Adorns and envelopes,

Like a glistening sea at dusk.

The creation, an artistic masterpiece

Which flows from thy mouth,

To establish this worldly canvas,

That enables the cascades of your glory.

May we — Always appreciate the splendor

Of thy word, thy glory and thy masterpiece.

That we may be adorned and enveloped

In your kingdom—that we may be like

The glistening sea at dusk.

Just as I AM

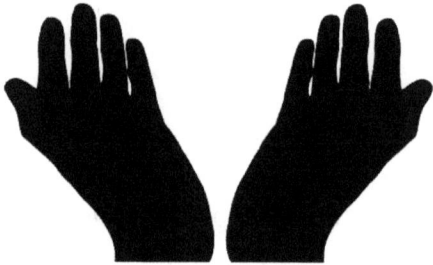

To me,

I am no-one,

A Mother serving, often lonely but for you.

To some

I am eccentric,

Strange, funny, misunderstood...

Haley Belinda / A Compilation

To you

My Lord and Saviour,

I am wonderful, beautifully adorned

like the princesses of old,

Made in your image,

forgiven and accepted.

Even though I am no-one;

To you,

I am everything

Just as I am.

Good Friday

Cursed and worn,

Wounded and torn

Still, you said, "Forgive them,

It is DONE. "White gowns adorned.

Amen!

God's Walk with Man

"*In* the first:

I walked the earth,

'For all of my friends.

To see"

"Secondly:

I sent my Son,

He came to set you free."

"Currently:

I am invisible,

to a world who's lost the plot!

Forgotten; with my voice and Love.

I actually made the lot."

"One day:

'Do Not Despair'

Keep the faith I will return.

I will reshape and mend,

This broken world"

Chapter 3-Family & Remembrance

Sweet Grandchild

A young lady called Ebony Rose,

Who liked to sing and to pose;

"Grandma, take out your camera,

I'm a 'ballerina"

Now she is pointing her toes!

Haley Belinda / A Compilation

For Riley...

Tomorrow is my grandsons

second Birthday party,

We will have lots of laughs

and they will be hearty,

Sandwiches, salads, sausages and cheese,

Oh, our little boy will be very pleased.

I know how excited he will be!

With the wrapping, the boxes

and all he will see!

The blocks, the trains, the million faces.

He's used to seeing them in different

places.

Happy Birthday, my little guy Riley,

I can't wait to see you all happy and smiley.

An Ode to my Dad. (His Life)

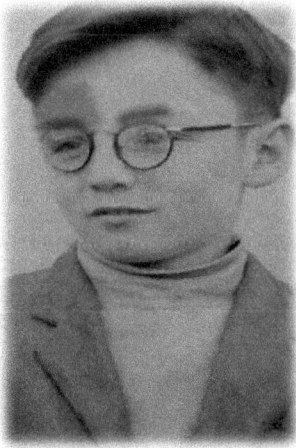

$\mathcal{L}$ike an orchid,

I blossomed away from my roots.

I thanked God for my flowers

I had produced.

Haley Belinda / A Compilation

My roots, although distant,

never did fade,

Our Brenda, Colin, Frank, Jack,

Sheila and Elaine.

This list is not exhausted,

I've left loads out.

My heart though,

never did without a doubt!

Born in PONTE, Castleford raised.

The navy became my travelling phase!

I marveled at Niagara as I watched the falls.

Then, back to ship for more of the world.

Next, I met Linda,

My love was she!

And before I knew it

We had three!

Three blossoms to nurture,

Each a different rose.

Now I was busy

In my humble abode.

Haley Belinda / A Compilation

I missed a vocation,

Boy, I could sing

and my hips shook like Elvis,

A Joy I did bring,

To all those I sang too from the heart.

Yes, I sang

just like a lark!

It wasn't all fun this journey of mine,

Spent time in the hospital,

That was a bind.

I left my mark though that is true,

I live in the many hearts of those I knew.

Now I am whole, completely pain-free

Sat in my mansion waiting for thee.

A Tale of Mother...

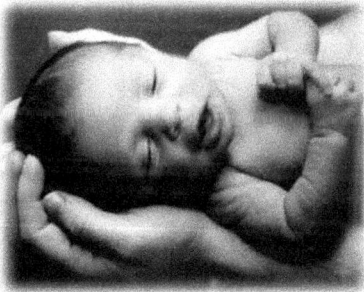

The soft peachy feel to your friendly face,

The lasting warmth of your cuddly embrace,

The tears roll down, as I recall,

The unconditional love of Mother.

Haley Belinda / A Compilation

The fine curls on my fingers

as I twisted your hair,

The bright yellow sun in my winters day,

Your resounding strength,

when I felt despair

The unconditional Love of Mother.

The spring in my step,

as I was encouraged

The sequins on my dresses,

from your hands of devotion,

I scream out with heartache,

full of emotion,

My wonderful comforting Mother

The unconditional love of my Mother.

Silent Despair

NB. The following poem is dedicated to
Mental Health awareness.

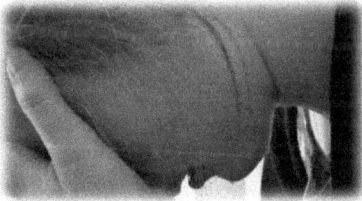

She's too young to sit in a cloud so black,

Wondering how she can fetch her way

back!

It's like a maze that she cannot get out,

"Away!" To her loved ones as she takes a

rant.

Desperately doing what some term
attention!
After the moment, it is not her intention.
It is a fit of frustration,
"I can't take anymore!"
As, she ushers her friends out of the door.

But that is not really what she wants;
Nor is 'the answer' at the forefront.
Prayer and care. That is the answer!
I will sit and wait for the miracle to save
her!
Thank YOU the miracle.

A Tribute to Dad

I know you would be proud of me

if you were here today!

Your smile, your grin, your jesting,

like me—On a good day!

Oh, Dad I really miss you and Mum.

At least you are together

and away from the 'hum drum'.

It's a different place without you!

All three of us agree!

Haley Belinda / A Compilation

Now I know your smiling,
"at last! It's how it should be!"

Just to reminisce, 'Do you remember
Shirley?'
The pink dress, the curls and ribbons,
in your boots on New Year's Eve?

I remember the day you took a trip!
Nope! It's not what you think!
You slid down the drive and
then disappeared.

We jumped out of the car and

to our surprise,

You were laid underneath

Thank God you were alright!

Yes, we have much to be thankful for,

The family, the fun and laughter,

If we had been filmed,

I'm sure we'd won a Bafta!

A Tribute to Mum

So, it passed,

Is it really a year?

Since the Mum we were blessed with,

Left us from here!

Back to the Father—Yes,

HE took you home,

but

We've mourned the loss of

our earthly backbone!

I am so thankful

to be born to you,

With your home sewn clothes

and 'The Yorkshire Stew!'

It's a fraction of the list

I could write here,

But, Mum

I will always miss you, DEAR.

Mum's Tribute 2 Years On

It is now two years,

How have I got through?
Not one day, could I forget you.
Not one hour, could I forget you.

It seems forever
since I touched your face
And you followed with a loving embrace.
And you hugged with a cuddly embrace.

I will pray to the end of my days;
I will stand behind you
In the garden of grace.
In the heavenly place.

There is one thing though,
that will make you smile?
I too had a chuckle
as the tear washed by,

I bet you are glad there
are no phones in His Mansion!
At least I cannot drive
you to distraction.

Sisterly Love...

From what I can remember,

Distant and true,

Happily, we played,

Both me and you.

Hopping round in anoraks,

Playing with mud stew!

We'd always have each other's backs,

Both me and you.

Back and forth we swung,

Singing on the ottoman,

Playing was such fun, for,

Both me and you.

Haley Belinda / A Compilation

You loved the horses,
I, the frilly dresses,
For tea, dip 'n' sauces,

For both you and me!

One day Mum disappeared,

Turned up in a bus,

It was a busy day, for,

Both you and me,

Our Mum she did call us,

It was half past three!

"Come see what I've got?"

Now we were three!

Grandma Saved My Day!

I went for a walk with Grandma

Grandma was the best you see!

See the shops in Shipley

Shipley a place near me

Me, I was a young teen.

'Teen that knew it all!

All that I saw coming

Coming before a fall.

Haley Belinda / A Compilation

Fall, not the Autumn kind,
Kind of, where one 'hits the ground,'
'Ground 'was a crossing with traffic lights
Lights that bleep and flash around.

Around the corner but near,
Near lights with rows of cars!
Cars that waited for us to cross
Cross over at the pedestrian place,
Place where I lost my underskirt
Underskirt full of lace.

The lace which should have stayed hidden.
Hidden beneath my dress!
'Dress which let go of it;
It left me embarrassed instead!

Instead of remaining decent
Decent and 'lady-like'!
Like a young blushing teen,
Teen that stood and cried.
Cried out to my Grandma,
"Grandma, what shall I do?"

"Do not look at the traffic"
'Traffic that is stealing a view!'
View of what was happening,
Happening to you.

You did the best you could,
Could you step out of it, now?
Now make light of it dear
Dear child, just shove it in here!

Haley Belinda / A Compilation

Here in my Grandma's Bag
Bag for the shopping in Shipley
Shipley, at last! Here we come,
Come on, love let's walk,
Walk on proudly, you and I-

I went for a walk with Grandma
Grandma was the best you see!
See the shops in Shipley
Shipley a place near me.

Chapter 4- Love.
A Soulmate or Lust-Mate?

My soulmate takes me to new heights.

We spent the night,

And half the day.

What can I say?

He said it had to stop today.

There as we lay,

This hurt me so,

I can't let go.

I thought he would come back one day?

Be here to stay,

It was the trust,

Must have been lust!

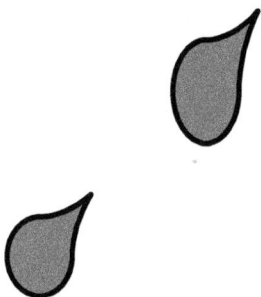

Waiting for love.

Long had I yearned for the sense of his

love,
Like a dove been set free, I had let him go

believing that we had fit hand in glove,

My heart kept faith with a constant glow,

The warmth of feeling his love is still there,

Even though you can't touch it,

that is hard to bear.

When I heard his story, I knew it matched

mine,

Soul to soul, my mate so divine.

He did not know this, as divulge I did not,

It sounded corny, like I'd copied his plot!

My dream was one day

that my prince would return,

To begin where we left off that day on the

phone.

I still think sometimes, that he is about.

Just certain notions, a feeling, then doubt.

I hope he is happy somewhere out there,

As happy as the feelings that I have

declared.

Will LOVE Be?

My heart feels sad,

I can relate,

I debate and wait,

Is it too late?

Years have gone by,

My dreams ran dry,

Our love though...

I could not deny!

My heart feels sad,

I cannot wait,

Would I see my love at the Pearly gate?

Please tell my heart,

It is NOT too late!

Come on Gods!

Be Awake!

My passion does burn,

I still do yearn,

The love I feel

I can't conceal,

Tell me, this isn't real?

My heart feels sad,

I cannot lie,

Would I have to wait until I die?

Oh no! Don't say it's not meant to be!

I cannot wait for eternity.

Perfect Love

Monogamous humans together

Compassionate feelings they share

Committed to each other's soul

Lasting love to declare

Never letting go

Hold me tightly

Show me hugs

Passion

Love

X

The End

Thank you for reading my poetry.

If, you enjoyed this book? Please, leave a
review where you purchased your copy to
enable me to produce more. For this I am
grateful.

If, you would like to see my continuing
works

follow me:

https://authorhaleybelinda.net

About the Author

Haley Belinda is an accomplished poet and

children's book author. During her lifetime

she has been a registered nurse (RGN) A

fitness instructor, a beauty therapist, salon

and nursing home manager. A wife, a

mother, a divorcee and now diagnosed with

Fibromyalgia she can finally concentrate on

her childhood secret to write.

Haley Belinda / A Compilation

Haley had ambitions to write a novel from secondary school, has been on the 'bucket list.' She discovered her poetic art by accident when at divorce it was the only way she could express her feelings.

Haley said, "As I open my heart to the readers, I hope they take solace, inspiration and enjoyment. This will then be the most important thing I ever achieved."

About the Book

Haley has been writing poetry since 2006 and this collection is a random selection of poems and tributes about family and other random occurrences.

You will find anything from Sonnets to Freestyle; therefore, it truly is a compilation for all.

www.ingramcontent.com/pod-product-compliance
Lightning Source LLC
Chambersburg PA
CBHW060040040426
42331CB00032B/1833